What is a My First Ac

- This book is a suitable size for children with small hands who are just starting to learn. They can apply stickers, color, and cut with scissors with ease.

- This small size allows children to look at each page without moving their eyes. They can easily understand the activity and remain engaged.

- For children on the go—they can enjoy this easy-to-carry format everywhere!

Features of
the Coloring Activity Book

This book contains a total of 126 coloring and drawing activities. It is designed to help children develop their skills in a more carefully calculated, step-by-step way. The coloring steps are as follows:

Level 1
Draw dots and lines freely without boundaries.

Level 2
Color a designated area with a designated color.

Level 3
Use colors that match the picture, or choose favorite colors.

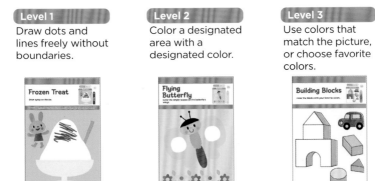

By following these steps, children will effortlessly develop fine motor skills to move their hands dexterously while using crayons. As they progress through the steps, their color recognition skills will also increase.

In addition, these activities include practice drawing short lines, long lines, curves, zigzags, and more. Children will develop the basic skills needed for writing letters as they progress. The latter half of the book includes pages for coloring freely to allow children to develop their creativity.

Fun-first activities build pen-control skills, color recognition, and creativity!

120+ kid-friendly coloring pages and 80+ stickers!

ACTIVITY BOOK

COLORING

MY FIRST

Play Smart

Gakken Workbooks

Ages 2+

Reward Stickers

Note to Parents

1) Most of the activities in this book should be at an appropriate developmental level, which will allow your child to do them independently. But don't hesitate to help them! When parents are involved in the learning process, it increases a child's intellectual curiosity and creates a more effective, supportive learning environment.

2) To support your child's learning, review the **"To Parents"** section featured below the instructions. These tips offer parents effective ways to explain the activity to your child.

3) As mentioned on the previous page, this book is divided into three steps. The first step, coloring freely, shifts to the second step, coloring in a specified place, but even then it does not matter if your child's coloring goes out of the frame. Prioritize the freedom to enjoy coloring rather than being exact about it. The repetition of these activities will lead to the next step. Another feature of this book is that the front and back sides are the same scene. The back side is slightly more difficult, offering more space to color than the front side. If the back side is difficult, your child can come back to do it later.

4) When your child finishes each activities, let them choose a **reward sticker** to put on the page. Be sure to also praise your child's good work! Be specific with your praise, saying something like, "You did a good job!" or "You were very patient!"

▌Hold a Crayon

Drawing Lines or Letters

Grip the crayon between your thumb and index finger, and then support it with your middle finger.

Coloring

Grip the top of the crayon firmly between your thumb and index finger.

▌How to Hold a Pencil

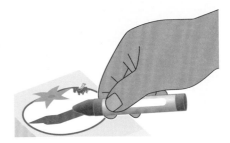

Hold the pencil at a 60-degree angle.

Hold the pencil just above the sharpened part. Be careful not to put too much pressure on your fingers.

Grip the pencil between your thumb and index finger, and then support it with your middle finger.

For writing practice, use a shorter, fatter pencil, as it is easier to grip.

Caution: The paper in this book can be sharp. Take care when handling. This book contains small stickers. Keep out of mouths.

Watermelon Seeds

Draw dots on the watermelon to add seeds.

Example

Black

To Parents Allow your child to hold the crayon however they want. You can show them how to make dots before they begin.

Watermelon Seeds

Draw more seeds.

Good
job!

Strawberry Seeds

Draw dots on the strawberries to add seeds.

Strawberry Seeds

Draw more seeds.

Playing in the Sand

Draw dots to add sand to the pile.

Example

Brown

Playing in the Sand

Draw more sand.

Good job!

Dad's Beard

Draw dots to finish Dad's beard.

Example

Black

To Parents | Learning to draw dots is similar to learning to draw short vertical lines. It's okay if some dots are a little longer than others.

Dad's Beard

Good job!

Draw more of Dad's beard.

Frozen Treat

Draw syrup on the ice.

To Parents Let your child draw however they want. It's okay if they mix horizontal lines, vertical lines, and diagonal lines. Using a crayon helps them develop fine motor skills and enriches their creativity.

Frozen Treat

Draw more syrup.

Good job!

Fluffy Clouds

Draw clouds in the sky.

White

Fluffy Clouds

Draw more clouds.

Red Tulip

Color the empty space on the flower.

Level 2 ★★☆

Example

Red

Red Tulip

Color one more flower.

Good job!

Green Leaf

Color the empty space on the leaf.

Example

Green

To Parents | Ask your child which color they should use to fill in the leaf.

Green Leaf

Color one more leaf.

Good
job!

Sweet Apple

Color the empty space on the apple.

Example

Red

Sweet Apple

Color one more apple.

Good job!

Delicious Bananas

Color the empty spaces on the bananas.

Delicious Bananas

Color more bananas.

Good
job!

Crisp Cucumbers

Color the empty spaces on the cucumbers.

Green

Crisp Cucumbers

Color more cucumbers.

Good job!

Flying Butterfly

Color the empty spaces on the butterfly's wings.

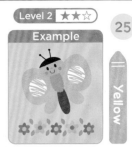

Example

Yellow

Flying Butterfly

Color more wings.

Good job!

Fresh Tomatoes

Color the empty spaces on the tomatoes.

Example

Red

Fresh Tomatoes

Color two more tomatoes.

Chirping Chicks

Color the empty spaces on the chicks.

Example

Yellow

Chirping Chicks

Color two more chicks.

Good job!

Watering Flowers

Draw lines to add more water.

Level 1 ★☆☆

Example

Light blue

To Parents This activity focuses on drawing straight lines. Show your child how to draw a line while saying, "Let's water the flowers!"

Watering Flowers

Draw more water.

Good job!

Falling Rain

Draw lines of rain.

Example

Light blue

To Parents   Encourage your child to hold the tip of their crayon, just like they would hold a pencil. This allows them to draw lines more easily. But remember not to force them.

Falling Rain

Draw more rain.

Good
job!

Puppy Race

Draw lines from 🔴 to 🔴.

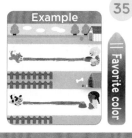
Example
Favorite color

To Parents | This activity challenges your child to draw a line from start to end in a designated area.

Puppy Race

Draw lines again.

Good job!

Fishing Fun

Draw fishing lines from ● to ●.

Example
Favorite color

Fishing Fun

Draw lines again.

Playful Sea Lions

Color the empty space of the ball.

To Parents | Encourage your child to color along the outline of the ball first. This will help them color within the ball.

Playful Sea Lions

Color two more balls.

Good job!

Crunchy Carrots

Color the carrot.

Crunchy Carrots

Color two more carrots.

Good job!

Cozy Socks

Color the sock.

Cozy Socks

Color two more socks.

Good job!

Orange Tree

Color the orange.

Example

Orange

Orange Tree

Color three more oranges.

Good
job!

Round Grapes

Color the grapes.

Example

Purple

Round Grapes

Color more grapes.

Good job!

Bear Buddies

Color the bear's face.

Example

Brown

Bear Buddies

Color one more bear.

Good job!

Striped Shirt

Draw horizontal lines on the shirt.

Example

Yellow

To Parents This activity practices drawing long horizontal lines. Encourage your child to draw each line to the end, even if it's shaky or uneven.

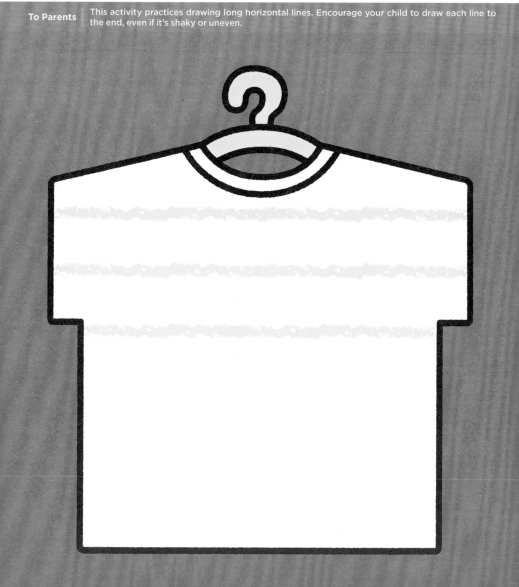

Striped Shirt

Draw more horizontal lines.

Good job!

Fancy Dress

Draw diagonal lines on the dress.

Example

Pink

To Parents | If it's difficult for your child to draw a diagonal line, place your hand on their hand to guide them.

Fancy Dress

Draw more diagonal lines.

Good job!

Striped Truck

Draw horizontal lines on the truck.

Example

Green

To Parents This activity allows your child to draw straight horizontal lines in larger areas. Encourage them to draw the lines closer together, so the space between them is narrow.

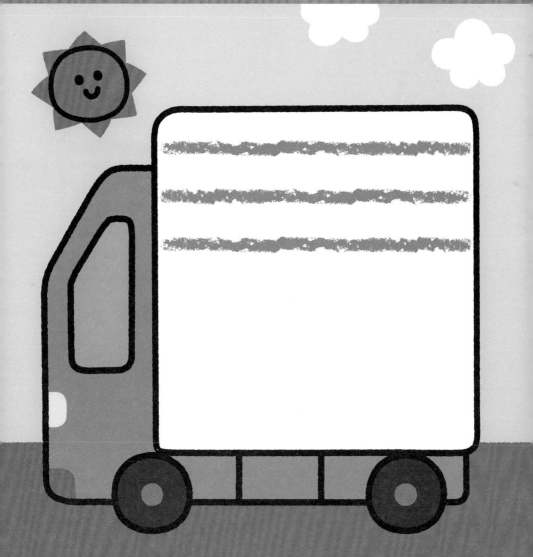

Striped Truck

Draw more horizontal lines.

Good job!

Sweet Melons

Draw vertical and horizontal lines on the melon.

Example

Green

Sweet Melons

Draw more lines.

Good job!

Walking Crabs

What color is a crab? Color it.

Example

Red

Walking Crabs

Color two more crabs.

Good
job!

Night Sky

What color are the moon and the star?
Color them.

Example

Yellow

Night Sky

Color one more moon and star.

Good job!

Speedy Fire Truck

What color is a fire truck? Color it.

Level 2 ★★☆

63

Example

Red

Speedy
Fire Truck

Color one more fire truck.

Good
job!

Lemon and Orange

What colors are the pieces of fruit?
Color them.

To Parents In this activity, your child will use two different colors. Before coloring, ask your child to name the colors of the lemon and the orange.

Lemon and Orange

Color more fruit.

Good job!

Lettuce and Green Pepper

What colors are the vegetables?
Color them.

Example

Green

Light green

Lettuce and Green Pepper

Good job!

Color more vegetables.

Bright Flowers

Color one flower's petals pink and
the other flower's center yellow.

Example

Yellow   Pink

To Parents   Ask your child what color they need to paint each part, referring to the example. When they are done coloring, praise your child by saying, "You made beautiful flowers."

Bright Flowers

Color more flowers.

Good job!

Summer Sunflower

Color the petals yellow and the leaf green.

Example

Green Yellow

Summer Sunflower

Color one more sunflower.

Good job!

Dinner Time

Draw dots to put food in the cat's dish.

Example

Brown

Snack Time

Draw more cat food.

Good job!

Dress-up Fun

Draw dots on the doll's outfit.

Example

Light blue

To Parents   This activity lets your child practice drawing dots at equal intervals. Refer to the girls in the example to draw.

Dress-up Fun

Draw more dots.

Good
job!

Rocket Launch

Example

Blue

Draw lines to add smoke.

Rocket Launch

Draw more smoke.

Good
job!

Under the Sea

Draw an ink cloud to hide the octopus from the shark.

Example

Black

To Parents   Before drawing, ask your child what they can draw for the octopus to keep the shark away.

Under the Sea

Draw more ink.

Good job!

Zoom Zoom

Draw lines from ● to ●.

Example

Favorite color

To Parents | After tracing the gray line, let your child connect the line to the blue point. It's okay if they can't draw straight.

Zoom Zoom

Draw more lines.

Good job!

Let's Take a Walk!

Draw lines from ● to ●.

Example

Favorite color

To Parents | Encourage your child to practice drawing lines, not only from top to bottom, but also from bottom to top.

Let's Take a Walk!

Draw more lines.

Good
job!

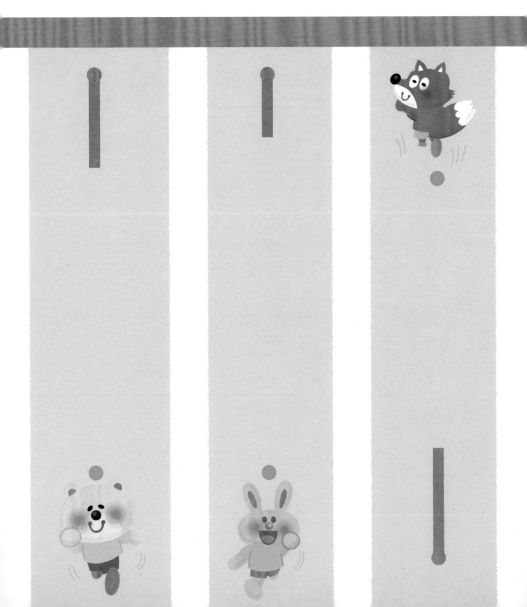

Zebra Stripes

Draw lines on the zebras.

Example

Black

Zebra Stripes

Draw more lines.

Good job!

Let's Go Home

Draw a continuous line from ● to ●.

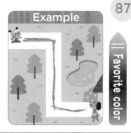
Example

Favorite color

To Parents | Tell your child to stop drawing when they need to change direction, then start again.

Let's Go Home

Draw another continuous line.

Good
job!

My Way Home

Draw a continuous line from 🔴 to 🔵.

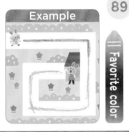

Example

Favorite color

To Parents It's important that your child learns to begin and end one continuous line. If it's difficult, encourage them to first trace the line with their finger and then draw the line.

My Way Home

Draw another continuous line.

Good job!

Sunny Flowers

Color the center of the flower.

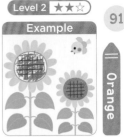

To Parents   Make sure your child practices coloring within the frame.

Sunny Flowers

Color one more flower.

Good
job!

Orange Juice

Color the juice.

Orange

Orange Juice

Color more juice.

Good job!

Cow Spots

Color the cow's spots.

Example

Black

Cow Spots

Color more spots.

Good job!

Tiger Pals

Color the tiger.

Tiger Pals

Color one more tiger.

Good job!

Jumping Frogs

Trace each line from ● to ●.

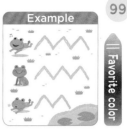
Example
Favorite color

Jumping Frogs

Trace more zigzag lines.

Good job!

Hopping Rabbits

Trace each line from ● to ●.

Example

Favorite color

To Parents Because it might be difficult to draw arched lines, allow your child to draw one semicircle at a time. If your child is having a hard time, place your hand on their hand for guidance.

Hopping Rabbits

Trace more arched lines.

Good job!

Puffy Clouds

Trace each line from ● to ●.

Example

Light blue

Puffy Clouds

Trace more clouds.

Good job!

Fluffy Sheep

Trace each line from ● to ●.

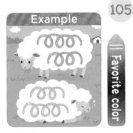

Example

Favorite color

To Parents | Drawing spiral lines is difficult because the motor function of your child's wrists and fingers are not fully developed. Encourage your child to draw slowly while putting your hand on theirs to help guide them.

Fluffy Sheep

Trace more spiral lines.

Good job!

A Ball of Yarn

Trace the line from  to ●.

Example

Blue

A Ball of Yarn

Trace one more spiral line.

Good
job!

Ice Cream Cones

Trace each line from ● to ●.

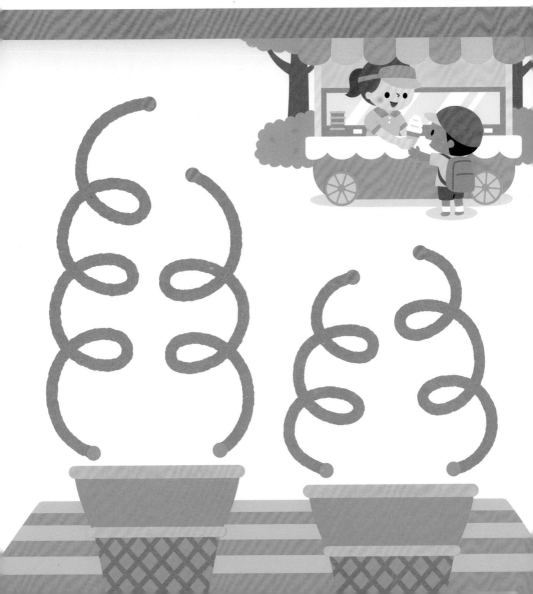

Ice Cream Cones

Trace more spiral lines.

Good job!

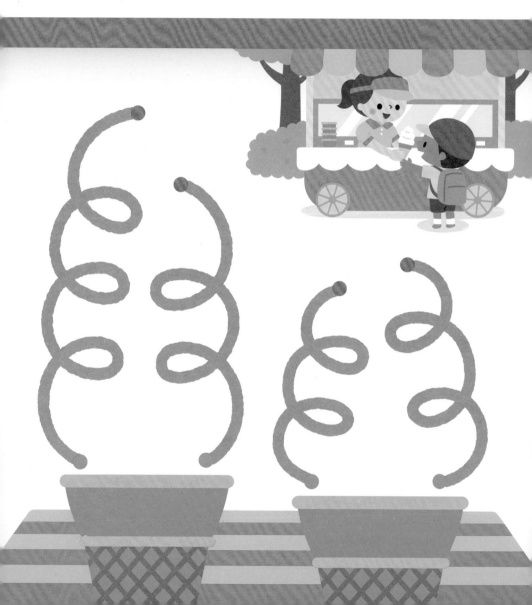

Spaghetti

Trace each line from  to .

Example

Orange

To Parents Draw together with your child while saying, "These noodles go around and around." When parents join in the activity, children become more motivated.

Spaghetti

Trace more spiral lines.

Good
job!

Big Trees

Color the empty triangles on the trees.

Example

Light green

To Parents | Have your child trace the outline of the white triangles, then color them.

Big Trees

Color two more trees.

Sunny-Side Up

Color the egg yolks.

Example

Yellow

To Parents Tell your child, "Make two fried eggs, please," and then let them color the yolks.

Sunny-Side Up

Color two more egg yolks.

Good job!

Colorful Balloons

Color the balloons with your favorite colors.

Example

To Parents Have your child choose their favorite colors. They can also select from the colors of the balloons in the illustration below.

Colorful Balloons

Color more balloons.

Good job!

Sailing the Seas

Color the boat's sails with your favorite colors.

Example

Favorite color

To Parents | Have your child trace the outlines of the white triangles, then color them.

Sailing the Seas

Good
job!

Color two more sails.

Pretty Hat

Color the hat with your favorite colors.

Example

Favorite color

Pretty Hat

Color one more hat.

Good job!

Warm Mittens

Color the mittens with your favorite color.

To Parents | It's okay to color each mitten with a different color. You can also draw a pattern first and then ask your child to color it.

Warm Mittens

Color two more mittens.

Good job!

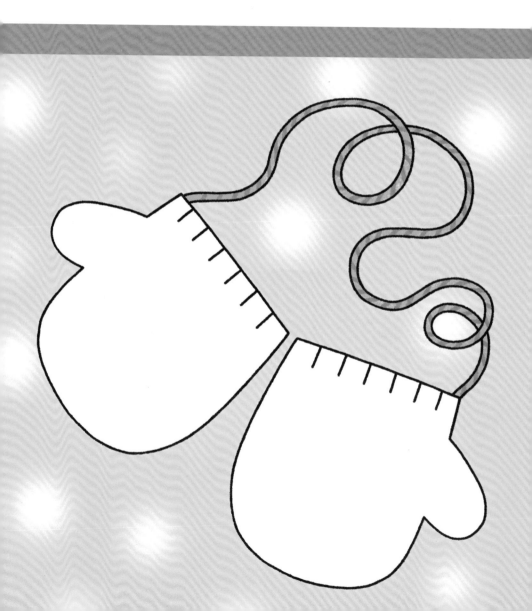

Building Blocks

Color the blocks with your favorite colors.

Building Blocks

Color more blocks.

Good job!

Fish Friends

Color the fish with your favorite colors.

Example

Favorite color

To Parents | Your child can also use different colors for the face and fins to make their own original fish.

Fish Friends

Color two more fish.

Good job!